MW01268289

Table of Contents

Cover figure illustration by: Tim Haggerty

John Wiley & Sons, Inc., founded in 1807, is an independent publishing company, publishing for the trade, professional, scientific, technical and educational marketplaces, with headquarters in New York City. In trade publishing, Wiley is best known in the areas of business and management, careers, computers, current affairs, biography, history, finance, investment, nature, science, psychology, tax, travel, and children's and young adult-nonfiction.

WILEY CHILDREN'S BOOKS

WELCOME TO THE WILEY CHILDREN'S CATALOG

Where children explore science and nature in the world around them.

Where inexpensive materials from around the house become
the stuff of great discoveries.

Where intriguing experiments at home and in the classroom
pave the way to lasting knowledge.

Where fascinating information combines with hands-on activities

for winning science fair projects.

And, best of all, where science is fun and learning is exciting!

12 new titles. 63 backlist titles.

And lots more in store for the coming seasons.

Take a look and discover Wiley Children's Books today!

Now kids everywhere can follow in the footsteps of America's first inventor.

THE BEN FRANKLIN BOOK OF EASY AND INCREDIBLE EXPERIMENTS

A FRANKLIN INSTITUTE SCIENCE MUSEUM BOOK

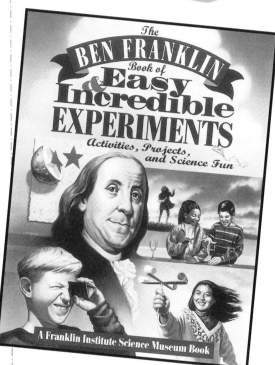

Every child knows the story of Ben Franklin and the kite and the key. But Franklin's scientific curiosity didn't stop there. His imagination led him to explore the weather, optics, printing, music, and more. To solve practical problems, he invented the lightning rod, the Franklin stove, and the first bifocal glasses. This spirit of inventiveness and hands-on experimentation continues today at Philadelphia's Franklin Institute Science Museum and in this inspiring book.

With this new book, young scientists everywhere can explore and enjoy science "Ben Franklin" style. From building a weather station with home-made barometers and hygrometers to creating an orchestra with panpipes, water chimes, and a shoe box guitar, **The Ben Franklin Book of Easy and Incredible Experiments** offers the kind of fun scientific inquiry that would make Ben proud.

★ **Explores the same topics that concerned Ben Franklin, including electricity, lenses and vision, music, and more**

★ **Includes some of Franklin's own experiments, plus other easy-to-do activities that continue from his explorations**

★ **Includes historical background on Franklin and his many science achievements**

THE FRANKLIN INSTITUTE SCIENCE MUSEUM (Philadelphia, Pennsylvania) is one of America's premier hands-on science museums. Founded with the help of Franklin himself, this world-renowned institution inspires the imaginations and investigative curiosity of millions of visitors every year.

- ■ National Publicity with Museum Spokesman
- ■ National Advertising
- ■ Co-promotions with Franklin Institute Science Museum
- ■ Special Consumer Offers

AUGUST

Paper
(0-471-07638-4)
$12.95 USA/$16.95 CAN
144 pp
8 1/2 x 11
100 Illustrations
Children/Science
Ages 8-12
Shipping: July 7
Cloth edition also available:
(0-471-07639-2)
$22.95* USA/$32.50* CAN

Fascinating projects—from fun &

EVERYDAY SCIENCE

Fun and Easy Projects for Making Practical Things

SHAR LEVINE AND LESLIE JOHNSTONE

For developing young minds, the everyday world is full of big mysteries.
How do telescopes make distant things look close up? What are rain-
bows made of? How can I keep my little sister out of my room? Now, in
this fun, fascinating science activities book written by popular children's
science author Shar Levine, kids (and their parents) get the scientific
explanations for these and dozens of other everyday mysteries while
learning how to make useful objects out of ordinary things.

- **Kids learn how to make a camera, a burglar alarm, a solar cooker, a barometer, and lots of other useful gizmos out of common household objects**

- **Covers projects in electricity and magnetism, heat and cold, light and optics, chemistry, earth science, and more**

- **Packed with fascinating and useful science facts and delightful illustrations**

MAY
Paper
(0-471-11014-0)
$9.95 USA/$12.95 CAN
96 pp.
8 1/8 X 8 1/4
100 Line Drawings
Children/Science
Ages 8-12
Shipping: April 14

practical to weird & wacky.

SILLY SCIENCE

Strange and Startling Projects to Amaze Your Family and Friends

SHAR LEVINE AND LESLIE JOHNSTONE

This book teaches serious science by giving kids plenty of what they love most—laughs! They'll be the envy of all the other kids on the block when, without the help of mirrors or hidden wires, they make spaghetti dance, make eggs flip in the air without touching them, and capture fruit in a bottle. And in the process they'll learn important scientific principles.

- **Kids learn how to make a potato maze, create a prehistoric "Spongesaurus," balance a fork on a glass, and many other tricks using ordinary household materials**

- **Includes activities that explain gravity, aerodynamics, nutrition, biology, chemistry, and more**

- **Illustrated with 100 amusing drawings and packed with goofy science facts and trivia**

SHAR LEVINE (Vancouver, British Columbia) is the former owner of Einstein's book and toy store and co-author of **Projects for a Healthy Planet** and **Einstein's Science Parties**. LESLIE JOHNSTONE (Vancouver, British Columbia) is an elementary school teacher and an editor of the journal of the British Columbia Teachers' journal, **Catalyst**.

MAY
Paper
(0-471-11013-2)
$9.95 USA/$12.95 CAN
96 pp.
8 1/8 X 8 1/4
100 Line Drawings
Children/Science
Ages 8-12
Shipping: April 14

Introducing...

What's the difference between a leopard and a jaguar?
What's the difference between jets and rockets?
What's the difference between frogs and toads?

Seemingly similar and often confused, these are just a few of the most baffling pairs in nature and science. Each of these reference books in the new *What's the Difference? Series* uses a collection of illustrated comparisons to explain the distinctions between everything from rabbits and hares to film and video.

➤ **Clear definitions in language a child can easily grasp are sprinkled throughout each book along with fun facts**

➤ **Entertaining writing style, easy-to-use format, and many illustrations combine to make learning fun**

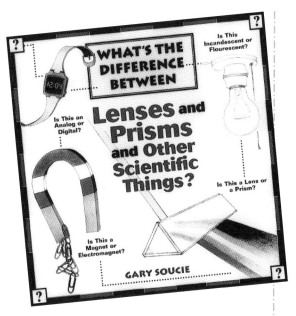

WHAT'S THE DIFFERENCE BETWEEN LENSES AND PRISMS AND OTHER SCIENTIFIC THINGS?

GARY SOUCIE

If adults find terms in science and technology a little confusing, think how much more daunting they can be for children. But this new book breaks concepts like radioactivity, mathematics, and magnetism into basic components and explains them through comparison. What's the difference between sound and noise, liquids and fluids, bits and bytes? These are just a few of the scientific marvels this book turns into child's play.

Explores the subjects that intrigue children the most: What makes things go? What is the invisible world inside machines and atoms like? and How do commonplace items like videotapes and CD-ROMs really work?

AUGUST
Paper
(0-471-08626-6)
$9.95 USA/$12.95 CAN
96 pp.
8 1/8 x 8 1/4
40 Illustrations
Children/Science
Ages 8 and up
Shipping: July 21

"What's the Difference?" Series

WHAT'S THE DIFFERENCE BETWEEN APES AND MONKEYS AND OTHER LIVING THINGS?

GARY SOUCIE

Children are fascinated by the natural world. They want to catch and collect bugs. Pick wild flowers. And they want to *know* about the living, breathing world around them. Each of the entries in this book covers a question any child might ask: What's the difference between hair and fur, horns and antlers, mushrooms and toadstools, seals and sea lions? As they enjoy exploring what makes similar living things different, they learn many of the most basic concepts of the life sciences.

Fully illustrated entries compare similar things in the plant and animal worlds and explain how they are different, including pollen and spores, stalks and stems, frogs and toads, and leopards and jaguars.

GARY SOUCIE (Cheverly, Maryland) was Executive Editor of **Audubon** magazine for more than 12 years. He has also served on the staff of **National Geographic** and written many articles on natural history.

AUGUST
Paper
(0-471-08625-8)
$9.95 USA/$12.95 CAN
96 pp
8 1/8 x 8 1/4
40 Illustrations
Children/Science
Ages 8 and up
Shipping: July 21

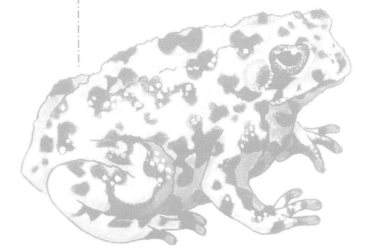

Great, new experiments from

Over 600,000 Science for Every Kid books sold!

JANICE VANCLEAVE'S THE HUMAN BODY FOR EVERY KID

Easy Activities that Make Learning Science Fun

JANICE VANCLEAVE

Of all the world's wonders, none is more fascinating than the human body. In this latest addition to the bestselling *Science for Every Kid Series*, everybody's favorite science teacher, Janice VanCleave, offers kids intriguing, easy-to-do activities that take the mystery out of how the body works—from making a model of the human skeleton to observing automatic balance responses to measuring reaction time.

 Dozens of activities on all the systems of the body, including the skeletal, muscular, and nervous systems

 All activities include simple, step-by-step directions, require only readily available materials, and are illustrated with lots of clear line drawings

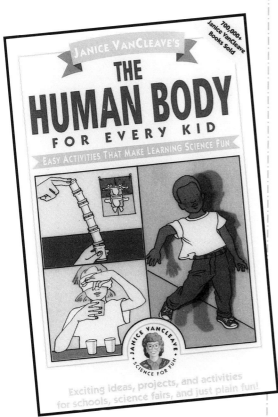

JANICE VANCLEAVE (Riesel, Texas) has a unique and always fun way of looking at science and brings this characteristic flair to every book. Janice taught science for 26 years, and is a popular presenter at museums, schools, and bookstores nationwide.

MARCH
Paper
(0-471-02408-2)
$10.95 USA/$14.95 CAN
240 pp.
6 x 9
100 Line Drawings
Children/Science
Ages: 8-12
Shipping: February 3
Cloth
(0-471-02413-9)
$24.95* USA/$34.95* CAN

- Coop Eligible
- Science For Every Kid Newsletter
- Teacher's Guide Available

Everyone's favorite science teacher.

JANICE VANCLEAVE'S WEATHER

Mind-Boggling Experiments You Can Turn Into Science Fair Projects

JANICE VANCLEAVE

Over 100,000 Spectacular Science Projects Series books sold!

Weather takes many fierce and beautiful forms, and just about all of them can be reproduced in the home or classroom. In this new addition to the popular *Spectacular Science Projects Series*, Janice VanCleave whisks kids right into the eye of the storm with easy-to-perform experiments that help them to understand how weather works and how meteorologists make sense of it. Why does it rain? What causes lightning and thunder? How do warm and cold fronts affect the weather? How do hurricanes form? What kids discover is sure to start their brains storming with great ideas for the best science projects ever!

- **20 easy-to-do experiments, plus dozens of tips and tricks for developing original science fair projects**

- **Activities include making a working barometer, building a hailstone, creating a cloud in a jar, and even performing the classic tornado experiment**

A SIGNATURE LOOK FOR JANICE VANCLEAVE!

The Janice VanCleave name is recognized by millions of children, teachers, and parents around the globe as a symbol of both quality education and science fun. For products that offer her signature blend of fun, science, and learning, just look for Janice's colorful logo.

MARCH
Paper
(0-471-03231-X)
$9.95 USA/$11.95 CAN
96 pp.
8 1/8 x 8 1/4
80 Line Drawings
Children/Science
Ages 8-12
Shipping: February 3

Makes working with numbers amazingly quick and simple!

ARITHMETRICKS

50 Easy Ways to Add, Subtract, Multiply, and Divide Without a Calculator

EDWARD H. JULIUS

When Ed Julius published his highly successful **Rapid Math Tricks and Tips** for adults, he discovered that kids were borrowing the book from their parents and becoming some of his biggest fans. Now he's written a totally new version of his astounding rapid math, especially for kids ages 10 to 15. **Arithmetricks** is packed with fifty tricks kids can use to add, subtract, multiply, and divide using simple short-cuts. Best of all, while they're entertaining themselves and their friends with amazing mathematical feats, young people will also be learning to feel comfortable and confident with numbers.

+ **Illustrations and a fun easy reading style appeal to a young audience**

+ **A great reference for parents and teachers who want to help children excel**

+ **Teaches kids how to do quick, accurate calculations in their heads, and helps prepare them for more advanced concepts**

JULY
Paper
(0-471-10639-9)
$10.95 USA/ $14.95 CAN
160 pp.
6 x 9
80 Illustrations
Children/Math
Ages 10-15
Shipping: June 23

EDWARD H. JULIUS (Chatsworth, California) is an award-winning professor of business administration at California Lutheran University. He lectures and conducts popular workshops on his rapid math methods for adults and young people.

Exciting, novel ways to make math interesting and relevant to kids' lives

MATH FOR THE VERY YOUNG

A Handbook of Activities for Parents and Teachers

LYDIA POLONSKY, DOROTHY FREEDMAN, SUSAN LESHER, AND KATE MORRISON

FOREWORD BY SHEILA SCONIERS AND MAX BELL
OF THE UNIVERSITY OF CHICAGO SCHOOL MATHEMATICS PROJECT

Experts recognize that math education should start early in a child's life. Parents are the primary teachers at this critical stage. Leaping ahead of simple counting books and tedious workbooks, this book offers hundreds of ideas for presenting math concepts to children ages 3 to 7 using the daily routines they share with parents. Familiar activities like cooking, doing laundry, going to the store, planning a party, or reading are used to introduce such age-appropriate concepts as counting, measuring, sorting, telling time, comparisons, and shapes and patterns.

- **Activities were developed in the spirit of the highly regarded University of Chicago School Mathematics Project (UCSMP)**

- **Concepts are easy enough that even the most math-wary parent will feel at ease teaching them**

- **Uses household items--from clocks, scales, and thermometers to books, cakes, and candles**

LYDIA POLONSKY, DOROTHY FREEDMAN, SUSAN LESHER, and KATE MORRISON are teachers who work for the University of Chicago School Mathematics Project.

MARCH
Paper
(0-471-01647-0)
$12.95 USA/$16.95 CAN
240 pp.
7 1/2 x 9 1/4
200 Drawings
Children/Math
Ages 3-7
Shipping: March 3
Cloth Edition also available (0-471-01671-3)
$22.95* USA/$32.50* CAN

Parenting

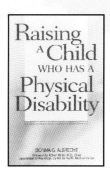

RAISING A CHILD WHO HAS A PHYSICAL DISABILITY

DONNA G. ALBRECHT
FOREWORD BY ROBERT MILLER, MD

Practical advice on every aspect of loving and living with a child with special needs

Here is encouraging and positive advice for parents on meeting the emotional, social, educational, recreational, and medical challenges of raising a child with a physical disability from infancy through the teen years. The author draws upon her personal experience with her own daughters to cover everything from dealing with medications, diet, and hygiene to developing positive self-esteem and choosing clothing. There is also advice on managing medical equipment and supplies, handling hospitalizations and emergencies, choosing a guardian, and finding long-term residential care. Throughout, the emphasis is on day-to-day living strategies and on helping the child who has special needs enjoy life to the fullest.

DONNA G. ALBRECHT (Concord, California) is a past president of the San Francisco Bay Area chapter of the Muscular Dystrophy Association. She also serves as a Peer Parent, a parent recommended by a physician to assist other parents in coping with the special needs of their children with physical disabilities.

APRIL   **Paper**   (0-471-04240-4)
$12.95 USA/$16.95 CAN
256 pp.   6 x 9
Children with Special Needs/Parenting
Shipping: March 17

CHILDHOOD SPEECH, LANGUAGE, AND LISTENING PROBLEMS

What Every Parent Should Know

PATRICIA McALEER HAMAGUCHI

How to tell if a child needs help—and where to get it

More than a million children aged 3 and up receive speech and language special education services in the U.S. This reassuring book enables parents who suspect something may be wrong to identify communication disorders that are often overlooked or misunderstood. Using simple descriptive terms, such as the "Him Not Talkin' Right" child, and the "I Forgot What You Said" child, the author explains what is considered "normal" for a child's development and tells parents what hidden warning signals to look out for. She describes the tests that will be conducted if a disorder is suspected and helps parents interpret the results.

> Helps to distinguish between a problem likely to be outgrown and one that requires outside help
> Outlines available options for speech and language therapy
> Provides activities parents can do at home to help their child progress

PATRICIA McALEER HAMAGUCHI (Brookfield, Connecticut) is a speech-language pathologist, certified by the American Speech-Language-Hearing Association. She currently practices in the Connecticut public schools.

MAY   **Paper**   (0-471-03413-4)
$12.95 USA/$16.95 CAN
224 pp.   6 x 9
Children with Special Needs/Parenting
Shipping: April 14

MATH FOR YOUR 1ST AND 2ND GRADER

All You Need to Know to be Your Child's Best Teacher

STEVE SLAVIN

An essential guide for parents who want to help their children learn

The fundamentals of mathematics—addition, subtraction, multiplication, and division—are all learned in the first crucial years of school. This illustrated, hands-on guide offers an easy way to be sure children master these basic skills. Based on the math curriculums of states across the country, it covers the fundamentals plus "new math" principles such as grouping. Simple activities reinforce each concept.

> 77 mini-lessons cover all the math required for first and second grades
> Shows parents how to be effective as teachers, including instructions on when to repeat a concept
> Includes a mastery test for each grade level
> An ideal resource for all concerned parents, including the over 500,000 homeschoolers nationwide

STEVE SLAVIN (Brooklyn, New York) is an economics and math professor at Union County College in New Jersey. He has written several textbooks and is the author of **All the Math You'll Ever Need** (also from Wiley) which has sold over 50,000 copies.

JUNE   **Paper**   (0-471-04242-0)
$12.95 USA/$16.95 CAN
256 pp.   7 1/2 x 9 1/4
Parenting/Math
Shipping: May 26

BestSellers—Wiley Children's Classics

Free Resources
for Teachers, Booksellers, and Librarians

THE JANICE VANCLEAVE TEACHER'S GUIDE

Packed with ideas for using VanCleave's Science for Every Kid and Spectacular Science Projects Series in the classroom. Available now for in-store promotions.

Ask your Sales Representative for details.

THE SCIENCE FOR EVERY KID CLUB

Thousands strong...and growing fast! Kids all across the country are catching on to the latest wave in science. They're joining the Science for Every Kid Club. Club members receive a free quarterly newsletter featuring science tidbits, games, and experiments. It's educational. It's exciting. And it's FREE!
Details in the back of each book.

THE JANICE VANCLEAVE SCIENCE FOR FUN INSTRUCTION KIT

Here is all you'll need to set up an in-store science extravaganza...Janice VanCleave style without Janice VanCleave. Includes helpful hints on how to set up, what materials you'll need, how to publicize the event, and of course, how to conduct the famous slime experiment without making a gooey mess of your store!

Ask your Sales Representative for details.

Children's

Janice VanCleave's SCIENCE FOR EVERY KID SERIES

Ages 8-12

Children everywhere have come to love these hands-on science books for their unique way of looking at the world through hundreds of safe, low-cost experiments. With Janice VanCleave, learning science is an exciting adventure!

Janice VanCleave's SPECTACULAR SCIENCE PROJECTS SERIES

Ages 8-12

Everyone's favorite science teacher offers fantastically fun answers to kids' annual question, "What can I do for the science fair this year?" Each book in this popular series includes 20 simple experiments on kids' favorite topics plus lots of ideas for exploring each topic further and developing them into the best science fair projects ever!

"Takes the beloved erupting volcano to new levels of exploration, ones that students will enjoy and science fair sponsors will accept."
—Booklist on **Janice Vancleave's VOLCANOES**

Janice VanCleave's
ASTRONOMY FOR EVERY KID
Paper (0-471-53573-7)
$10.95 USA/$14.95 CAN
240 pp. 6 x 9 1991
Library Edition:
(0-471-54285-7)
$24.95* USA/$34.95* CAN

Janice VanCleave's
BIOLOGY FOR EVERY KID
Paper (0-471-50381-9)
$10.95 USA/$14.95 CAN
240 pp. 6 x 9 1990
Library Edition:
(0-471-51048-3)
$24.95* USA/$34.95* CAN

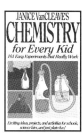

Janice VanCleave's
CHEMISTRY FOR EVERY KID
Paper (0-471-62085-8)
$10.95 USA/$14.95 CAN
240 pp. 6 x 9 1989
Cloth: (0-471-50974-4)
$22.95*USA/$32.50* CAN

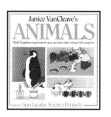

Janice VanCleave's
ANIMALS
Paper (0-471-55052-3)
$9.95 USA/$11.95 CAN
96 pp. 8 1/8 x 8 1/4 1992

Janice VanCleave's
EARTHQUAKES
Paper (0-471-57107-5)
$9.95 USA/$11.95 CAN
96 pp. 8 1/8 x 8 1/4 1993

Janice VanCleave's
ELECTRICITY
Paper (0-471-31010-7)
$9.95 USA/$11.95 CAN
96 pp. 8 1/8 x 8 1/4 1994

Janice VanCleave's
DINOSAURS FOR EVERY KID
Paper (0-471-30812-9)
$10.95 USA/$14.95 CAN
240 pp 6 x 9 1994
Cloth: (0-471-30813-7)
$24.95* USA/$34.95* CAN

Janice VanCleave's
EARTH SCIENCE FOR EVERY KID
Paper (0-471-53010-7)
$10.95 USA/$14.95 CAN
240 pp. 6 x 9 1991
Library Edition:
(0-471-54389-6)
$24.95* USA/$34.95* CAN

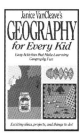

Janice VanCleave's
GEOGRAPHY FOR EVERY KID
Paper (0-471-59842-9)
$10.95 USA/$14.95 CAN
240 pp. 6 x 9 1993
Cloth: (0-471-59841-0)
$24.95* USA/$34.95* CAN

Janice VanCleave's
GRAVITY
Paper (0-471-55050-7)
$9.95 USA/$11.95 CAN
96 pp. 8 1/8 x 8 1/4 1992

Janice VanCleave's
MACHINES
Paper (0-471-57108-3)
$9.95 USA/$11.95 CAN
96 pp. 8 1/8 x 8 1/4 1993

Janice VanCleave's
MAGNETS
Paper (0-471-57106-7)
$9.95 USA/$11.95 CAN
96 pp. 8 1/8 x 8 1/4 1993

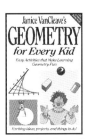

Janice VanCleave's
GEOMETRY FOR EVERY KID
Paper (0-471-31141-3)
$10.95 USA/$14.95 CAN
240 pp. 6 x 9 1994
Cloth: (0-471-31142-1)
$24.95* USA/$34.95* CAN

Janice VanCleave's
MATH FOR EVERY KID
Paper (0-471-54265-2)
$10.95 USA/$14.95 CAN
240 pp. 6 x 9 1991
Library Edition:
(0-471-54693-3)
$24.95* USA/$34.95*CAN

Janice VanCleave's
PHYSICS FOR EVERY KID
Paper (0-471-52505-7)
$10.95 USA/$14.95 CAN
240 pp. 6 x 9 1991
Library Edition:
(0-471-54284-9)
$24.95* USA/$34.95* CAN

Janice VanCleave's
MICROSCOPES AND MAGNIFYING LENSES
Paper (0-471-58956-X)
$9.95 USA/$11.95 CAN
96 pp. 8 1/8 x 8 1/4 1993

Janice VanCleave's
MOLECULES
Paper (0-471-55054-X)
$9.95 USA/$11.95 CAN
96 pp. 8 1/8 x 8 1/4 1992

Janice VanCleave's
VOLCANOES
Paper (0-471-30811-0)
$9.95 USA/$11.95 CAN
96 pp. 8 1/8 x 8 1/4 1994

Backlist

TWO VANCLEAVE SCIENCE BONANZAS FEATURE HUNDREDS OF EXPERIMENTS THAT SPAN THE WHOLE SCIENCE WORLD...

Ages 8-12

JANICE VANCLEAVE'S 200 GOOEY, SLIPPERY, SLIMY, WEIRD, AND FUN EXPERIMENTS
Paper (0-471-57921-1)
$12.95 USA/$15.95 CAN
128 pp. 8½ x 11 1992

JANICE VANCLEAVE'S 201 AWESOME, MAGICAL, BIZARRE, AND INCREDIBLE EXPERIMENTS
Paper (0-471-31011-5)
$12.95 USA/$15.95 CAN
128 pp. 8½ x 11 1994

THE FLYING START SCIENCE SERIES

Ages 8-12
KIM TAYLOR

"Splendid color photos...Engrossing and exciting...Transforms science from word or curriculum to the real world around us."
—Kirkus

Combining four-color action photographs, bold graphics, and intriguing ideas and experiments, this series offers children a powerful and compelling vision of the science around them.

  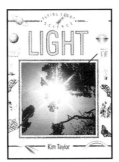

ACTION
Cloth (0-471-57193-8)
$12.95 USA/$18.50 CAN
32 pp. 8½ x 11 1992

FLIGHT
Cloth (0-471-57983-1)
$12.95 USA/$18.50 CAN
32 pp. 8½ x 11 1992

LIGHT
Cloth (0-471-57192-X)
$12.95 USA/$18.50 CAN
32 pp. 8½ x 11 1992

  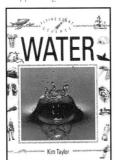

PATTERN
Cloth (0-471-57982-3)
$12.95 USA/$18.50 CAN
32 pp. 8½ x 11 1992

STRUCTURE
Cloth (0-471-57195-4)
$12.95 USA/$18.50 CAN
32 pp. 8½ x 11 1992

WATER
Cloth (0-471-57194-6)
$12.95 USA/$18.50 CAN
32 pp. 8½ x 11 1992

THE LOOKING AT...SERIES

Ages 8-12
DAVID SUZUKI

96 pp.   8¼ x 8¼   **Children/Science**   No Canadian rights

The host of the popular TV science show "The Nature of Things" introduces science to children with simple, step-by-step activities as well as amazing facts and illustrations.

LOOKING AT THE BODY
Paper (0-471-54052-8)
$9.95   1991
Library Edition
(0-471-54752-2) $22.95*

LOOKING AT THE ENVIRONMENT
Paper (0-471-54051-X)
$9.95   1991
Library Edition
(0-471-54749-2) $22.95*

LOOKING AT INSECTS
Paper (0-471-54050-1)
$9.95   1991
Library Edition
(0-471-54747-6) $22.95*

LOOKING AT PLANTS
Paper (0-471-54049-8)
$9.95   1991
Library Edition
(0-471-54748-4) $22.95*

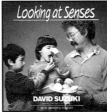 

LOOKING AT SENSES
Paper (0-471-54048-X)
$9.95   1991
Library Edition
(0-471-54751-4) $22.95*

LOOKING AT WEATHER
Paper (0-471-54047-1)
$9.95   1991
Library Edition
(0-471-54753-0) $22.95*

Children's Backlist

THE OCEAN BOOK
Aquarium and Seaside Activities and Ideas for All Ages
THE CENTER FOR MARINE CONSERVATION

A wide range of educational and fun experiments, investigations, and puzzles take children deep into the mystery and grandeur of the seas and place a special emphasis on the conservation of endangered species.

Paper (0-471-62078-5)
$12.95 USA/$16.95 CAN
128 pp. 8½ x 11 1989
ages 5-12

THE EARTH SCIENCE BOOK
Activities for Kids
DINAH ZIKE

Providing a simple, scientific look at basic earth science concepts and timely environmental issues, this book helps children uncover secrets about the Earth's composition, movement, oceans, atmosphere, habitats, and environment.

Paper (0-471-57166-0)
$12.95 USA/$16.95 CAN
128 pp. 8½ x 11 1993
ages 8-12

EARTH-FRIENDLY TOYS
How to Make Fabulous Toys and Games from Reusable Objects
GEORGE PFIFFNER

"After a useful introduction on measuring, cutting, and transferring patterns, Pfiffner clearly explains how to make a variety of toys that can be used in games or entertainments, including toys that move."
—Booklist

Build a castle from old oatmeal boxes and toilet paper rolls. Craft a fleet of paddle boats out of discarded styrofoam. These are just a few of the 30 different projects in **Earth-Friendly Toys**. Also includes facts about recycling and conservation.

Paper (0-471-00822-2)
$12.95 USA/$16.95 CAN
128 pp. 11 x 8½ 1994
Ages 8-12

EARTH-FRIENDLY WEARABLES
How to Make Fabulous Clothes and Accessories from Reusable Objects
GEORGE PFIFFNER

Dress up in style in the second installment in the *Earth-Friendly Series*. 30 imaginative craft projects for making belts, bracelets, bags, and hats out of reusable materials.

Paper (0-471-00823-0)
$12.95 USA/$16.95 CAN
128 pp. 11 x 8½ 1995
ages 8-12

GET GROWING!
Exciting Indoor Plant Projects for Kids
LOIS WALKER

This book teaches children how to grow their own fruits and vegetables indoors and offers exciting craft projects and recipes.

Paper (0-471-54488-4)
$9.95 USA/$13.95 CAN
104 pp. 8½ x 10 1991
ages 5-10

PET BUGS
A Kids' Guide to Catching and Keeping Touchable Insects
SALLY KNEIDEL

"The clear and direct title...doesn't really convey just how much can be learned here..."
—Booklist

This interactive guide explains exactly how to find and keep approximately 25 common insects that are safe to touch and fun to watch!

Paper (0-471-31188-X)
$10.95 USA/$14.95 CAN
128 pp. 7 x 10 1994
ages 8-12

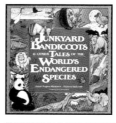

JUNKYARD BANDICOOTS & OTHER TALES OF THE WORLD'S ENDANGERED SPECIES
JOYCE ROGERS WOLKOMIR AND RICHARD WOLKOMIR

In this delightfully illustrated story book, kids meet many of the world's endangered species close up and discover amazing details about these creatures and their habitats.

Paper (0-471-57261-6)
$9.95 USA/$13.95 CAN
112 pp. 8 x 8 1992
ages 8-12

PROJECTS FOR A HEALTHY PLANET
Simple Environmental Experiments for Kids
SHAR LEVINE AND ALLISON GRAFTON

Combining interesting projects with information about today's environmental concerns, this book offers a fun way to teach children about the environment and shows how they can make a difference in caring for it.

Paper (0-471-55484-7)
$10.95 USA/$13.95 CAN
96 pp. 8 x 8 1992
ages 8-12

Young Adult Titles

NATURE IN A NUTSHELL FOR KIDS
Over 100 Activities You Can Do In Ten Minutes or Less
JEAN POTTER

Here's a fascinating and interactive way for kids to explore the natural world—from how plants and animals grow to how rivers and mountains are formed.

Paper (0-471-04444-X)
$10.95 USA/$14.50 CAN
144 pp. 8⅛ x 8¼ 1995
ages 8-12

SCIENCE IN SECONDS FOR KIDS
Over 100 Experiments You Can Do in Ten Minutes Or Less
JEAN POTTER

A veritable science feast in bite-size portions, this treasury of quick and easy experiments spans the science curriculum.

Paper (0-471-04456-3)
$10.95 USA/$14.50 CAN
144 pp. 8⅛ x 8¼ 1995
ages 8-12

NATURE FOR THE VERY YOUNG
A Handbook of Indoor and Outdoor Activities
MARCIA BOWDEN

This lively handbook of inventive and entertaining activities emphasizes basic concepts of color recognition, sequencing, and body awareness.

Paper (0-471-62084-X)
$12.95 USA/$18.50 CAN
242 pp. 7 x 10 1989
Cloth (0-471-50975-2)
$22.95 USA/$32.50 CAN
Parents' Guide for Children Ages 3-7

ROLLER COASTER SCIENCE
50 Wet, Wacky, Wild, Dizzy Experiments About Things Kids Love Best
JIM WIESE

Why does a Frisbee fly? Why don't you fall out of amusement park rides when they go upside down? Using a series of fun experiments, Jim Wiese offers the intriguing answers to these and other questions about the things kids love best.

Paper (0-471-59404-0)
$12.95 USA/$16.95 CAN
128 pp. 7 x 10 1994
ages 8-12

THE CURIOSITY CLUB
Kids' Nature Activity Book
ALLENE ROBERTS

A multitude of simple and fun-filled activities reveals the beauty and excitement of the natural world to children.

Paper (0-471-55589-4)
$14.95 USA/$19.95 CAN
160 pp 8½ x 11 1992
ages 6-12

THE SCIENCE CHEF
100 Fun Food Experiments and Recipes for Kids
JOAN D'AMICO AND KAREN EICH DRUMMOND

Why do onions make you cry? How does bread rise? What makes popcorn pop? The Science Chef serves up the answers to these and many other fascinating questions with recipes that are both fun cooking projects and intriguing experiments demonstrating scientific principles.

Paper (0-471-31045-X)
$12.95 USA/$16.95 CAN
192 pp. 7 ½ x 9¼ 1994
ages 8-14

BEST SCIENCE PROJECTS FOR YOUNG ADULTS
Ages 12 and up

This exciting series offers young scientists ages 12 and up stimulating experiment ideas that don't require expensive or unusual equipment. Guaranteed to inspire the imagination of emerging scientists everywhere!

ANIMAL BEHAVIOR SCIENCE PROJECTS
NANCY WOODARD CAIN

Welcome news! Science projects on animal behavior that are harmless to animals.
Paper (0-471-02636-0)
$12.95 USA/$18.50 CAN
160 pp. 7 x 10 1995
ages 12 and up

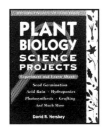

PLANT BIOLOGY SCIENCE PROJECTS
DAVID R. HERSHEY

A collection of complete science fair projects on one of today's most requested topics.
Paper (0-471-04983-2)
$12.95 USA/$18.50 CAN
160 pp. 7 x 10 1995
ages 12 and up

JANICE VANCLEAVE'S A+ PROJECTS
Ages 12 and up

Bestselling science author Janice VanCleave brings her unique brand of science inquiry to junior high and high school students. Each book features 30 experiment ideas with background information and ideas for further investigation.

JANICE VANCLEAVE'S A+ PROJECTS IN BIOLOGY
Paper (0-471-58628-5)
$12.95 USA/$16.95 CAN
240 pp. 6 x 9 1993
Cloth: (0-471-58629-3)
$22.95*USA/$32.50* CAN

JANICE VANCLEAVE'S A+ PROJECTS IN CHEMISTRY
Paper (0-471-58630-7)
$12.95 USA/$16.95 CAN
240 pp. 6 x 9 1993
Cloth: (0-471-58631-5)
$22.95* USA/$32.50* CAN

Young Adult Titles

THE COMPLETE HANDBOOK OF SCIENCE FAIR PROJECTS

JULIANNE BOCHINSKI

This idea-packed handbook provides guidance in preparing over 50 award-winning projects, plus a list of 500 other suggested topics.
Paper (0-471-52728-9)
$12.95 USA/$18.50 CAN
224 pp.   7 x 10   1991
ages 12-16
Cloth: (0-471-52729-7)
$29.95*USA/$41.95*CAN

THE HOUSE OF SCIENCE

PHILIP R. HOLZINGER

As young adults wander through the rooms of this extraordinary house, they become acquainted with the various sciences.
Paper (0-471-50061-5)
$15.95 USA/$22.50 CAN
238 pp.   7 x 10   1990
ages 10-14

THE FASCINATING FRESH WATER FISH BOOK

How to Catch, Keep, and Observe Your Own Native Fish
JOHN R. QUINN

This book takes young people into the world of native fish living in local rivers, creeks, ponds, and lakes.
Paper (0-471-58601-3)
$10.95 USA/$14.95 CAN
160 pp.   7 x 10   1994
ages 10-15

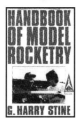

HANDBOOK OF MODEL ROCKETRY

Sixth Edition
G. HARRY STINE

Here's everything you need to know about enjoying one of today's hottest hobbies. The official handbook of the National Association of Rocketry.
Paper (0-471-59361-3)
$17.95 USA/$24.50 CAN
384pp.   6⅛x9¼   1994
ages 12 and up

TELESCOPE POWER

Fantastic Activities and Easy Projects for Young Astronomers
GREGORY MATLOFF

A host of simple educational activities makes astronomy fun and easy.
Paper (0-471-58039-2)
$12.95 USA/$18.50 CAN
128 pp.   7 x 10   1993
ages 10-15

STUDENT SCIENCE OPPORTUNITIES

Your Guide to Over 300 Exciting National Programs, Competitions, Internships, & Scholarships
GAIL GRAND

A resource directory listing incredible science opportunities for junior high and high school students, plus programs for others from age 8 through adult.
Paper (0-471-31088-3)
$14.95 USA
304 pp.   6 x 9   1994
ages 14 and up
No Canadian Rights

LUCKY SCIENCE

Accidental Discoveries from Gravity to Velcro, with Experiments!
ROYSTON ROBERTS AND JEANIE ROBERTS

Historical anecdotes and fun experiments teach kids about some of science's serendipitous discoveries.
Paper (0-471-00954-7)
$10.95 USA/$14.95 CAN
128 pp.   7 x 10   1994
ages 10-15

THE THOMAS EDISON BOOK OF EASY & INCREDIBLE EXPERIMENTS

Activities, Projects, and Science Fun for All Ages
THE THOMAS ALVA EDISON FOUNDATION

Reflecting Edison's fascination with experimentation, this book is packed with a range of experiments and projects.
Paper (0-471-62090-4)
$12.95 USA/$18.50 CAN
160 pp.   8½ x 11   1988
ages 10-14
Cloth (0-471-62089-0)
$24.95 USA/$34.95 CAN

Parenting Backlist

CHINESE BRAIN TWISTERS

50 Fast, Fun Puzzles that Teach Children How to Think
BAIFANG

Passed down by generations of Chinese parents, these mental calisthenics offer an interesting and smart way to help kids learn to think logically and creatively.
Paper (0-471-59505-5)
$12.95 USA/$16.95 CAN
128 pp.   6 x 9   1994

HYPERACTIVITY

SAM GOLDSTEIN AND MICHAEL GOLDSTEIN

A commonsense approach to understanding the medical and non-medical maze of evaluation and treatment, and successfully managing the problems of hyperactive children.
Paper (0-471-53307-6)
$12.95 USA/$16.95 CAN
256 pp.   5½ x 8⅜   1993

TAMING THE DRAGON IN YOUR CHILD

Solutions for Breaking the Cycle of Family Anger
MEG EASTMAN

A child and family psychologist offers effective strategies for dealing with children's anger—from toddlerhood through adolescence.
Paper (0-471-59405-9)
$14.95 USA/$19.95 CAN
256 pp.   6 x 9   1994

EINSTEIN'S SCIENCE PARTIES

Easy Parties for Curious Kids
SHAR LEVINE AND ALLISON GRAFTON

A unique party planner with ideas for a host of intriguing science theme parties—from an I Spy party with invisible ink made from lemon juice to zany experiments you can eat.
Paper (0-471-59646-9)
$10.95 USA/$14.95 CAN
96 pp.   8¼ x 8¼   1994

LOVE AND POWER

GLENN AUSTIN

This wise and practical book counsels parents on ways to resolve power conflicts with their children while empowering them and enhancing their self-esteem.
"Great job."   —T. Berry Brazelton, MD
Paper (0-471-02498-8)
$12.95 USA/$16.95 CAN
272 pp.   6 x 9   1994

*Titles with an asterisk are short discounted

Author Index

Trade Sales Representatives

TOM CARNEY
Regional Sales Manager
Tel: (303) 423-4111
Fax: (303) 422-2463
Colorado; Wyoming

GEORGE CARROLL
Tel: (508) 477-1296
Fax: (508) 477-1531
New Hampshire; Maine;
Eastern Massachusetts;
Rhode Island;
Eastern Connecticut

EARL COX
Tel: (718) 379-0991
Fax: (718) 379-5361
New York City

LISA D'ARPA
National Accounts
Regional Sales Manager
(212) 850-6284

DIANE DOOLEY
(609) 799-6396
Central & Southern New Jersey;
Eastern Pennsylvania; Delaware;
Baltimore; Northern Maryland

ROBERT DYER
(913) 631-7706
Indiana; Iowa; Kansas;
Missouri; Nebraska; New Mexico;
North Dakota; South Dakota;
El Paso, Texas

RICHARD FOX
Tel/Fax: (404) 971-6089
Alabama; Florida; Georgia; North
Carolina; Mississippi;
South Carolina; Tennessee

JOEL GEILS
National Accounts
(212) 850-6122

DENNIS GRESH
Tel/Fax: (216) 521-3529
Richmond, Indiana; Kentucky;
Michigan; Ohio; Southwest
West Virginia

ROBERT KUHNER
Tel: (714) 768-1545
Fax: (714) 583-0704
Arizona; Southern California; Hawaii;
Nevada (except Reno)

STEPHANIE MAKOWKA
Tel/Fax: (203) 967-8721
Southern Connecticut; Maryland;
Northern New Jersey;
Westchester County, New York;
Virginia; Washington DC

SAL McLEMORE
Tel/Fax: (713) 360-5204

ELIDA TAMEZ
(817) 382-5384
Arkansas; Louisiana; Oklahoma;
Texas (except El Paso)

WILLIAM POISSON
Tel: (415) 621-7660
Fax: (415) 861-5153
Northern California;
Reno, Nevada

SHELLEY SANTA
(708) 397-0947
Illinois; Northern Indiana;
Minnesota; Wisconsin

SANDY SIEGLE
(206) 524-6530
Alaska; Idaho; Montana; Oregon;
Utah; Washington

ELIZABETH STEINGRABER
Sales Manager—Professional Books
Tel: (301) 840-9074
Fax: (301) 869-1396

DIXIE WALKER
(607) 387-7005
Northern Connecticut; New York
(north of Rockland County);
Western Massachusetts;
Western Pennsylvania; Vermont

Library Sales Representatives

JOHN CHAMBERS
Director-Library Sales
John Wiley & Sons, Inc.
605 Third Avenue
New York, NY 10158
(212) 850-6291

BARRY CHAMPANY
West Coast
70 Vicente Road
Berkeley, CA 94705
(510) 548-6179

ATHENA MICHAEL
East Coast
705 Woodland Avenue
Winchester, VA 22601
(703) 722-0523

Latin American Sales Representatives

LAURIE RUBIN, Regional Manager
Latin American Sales Dept.
John Wiley & Sons, Inc.
605 Third Avenue
New York, NY 10158
Tel: (212) 850-6464
Fax: (212) 850-6019
Latin America

MICHAEL BATES
Rua das Palmeiras, 32 Apto. 701
22270 Rio de Janeiro, RJ
Brazil
Tel: 011-55-21-286-8951
Fax: 011-55-21-537-2578
South America

ROBERT BLAKE
Apartado Postal 41-533
Mexico 11000, D. F. Mexico
Tel/Fax: 011-525-544-3587
Mexico & Central America

ROSARIO PIETRI, Sales Representative
John Wiley & Sons, Inc.
Calle Sabila W14
Urb. Santa Clara
Guaynabo, Puerto Rico 00969
Tel/Fax: (809) 731-5098
Puerto Rico & the Caribbean